WASI

A Handbook of Japanese Food

Preface

Japanese cuisine, or *washoku*, is more than just food on a plate. Deeply rooted in the country's cultural heritage, it offers a window into Japan's rich traditions and reflects the Japanese people's connection to nature and the changing seasons. Known for its meticulous attention to detail and delicate balance of flavors, textures, and presentation, Japanese food is a feast for both the stomach and the eyes.

In recent years, interest in Japanese culture and cuisine has flourished around the world, with foods such as *gyoza* and *mochi* becoming readily available in supermarkets and on restaurant menus. "*Umami*," which is sometimes translated as the "essence of deliciousness," has become a buzzword and is now often referred to as the fifth taste, in addition to sweet, sour, salty, and bitter. Naturally found in foods such as mushrooms, cheese, and soy sauce, *umami* is a central concept of Japanese cooking, shaping and enhancing the flavors of many dishes.

From the skilled craftsmanship of sushi to the warm comfort of *ramen*, experiencing the food is a highlight for many visitors to Japan. But for first-timers, ordering unfamiliar dishes at restaurants can sometimes feel daunting. Of course, there's more to Japanese food than just sushi or Kobe beef served in high-end restaurants. Japan boasts a wide range of eateries, including those serving *B-kyu gurume*. Literally translated as "B-rank food," these are the meals of everyday Japanese people. Curry rice, *oyakodon*, and *yakisoba* are all comfort foods that can be found everywhere at a reasonable price. Whether you're enjoying a meal with friends in a casual *izakaya* or experiencing an elaborate *kaiseki* meal in a guesthouse, you'll find a wealth of dishes to explore.

In this book, we'll take you through different types of Japanese food and introduce lesser-known regional specialties. You can even learn what Japanese cooks use to give *washoku* its unique taste in the "Secret Ingredients" section.

As you explore the pages ahead, remember that *washoku* is as much about the experience as it is about the flavors. It's about sitting shoulder to shoulder with office workers and taking the first sip of broth at a hole-in-the-wall *ramen* joint. It's about admiring the exquisite presentation of a selection of Japanese sweets next to a beautiful bowl of green tea. It's about choosing dishes to share with friends as you unwind at the end of a long day.

We hope that you enjoy your adventures in Japanese cuisine, and don't forget to say *"itadakimasu"* before you dig in!

Raina Ruth Nakamura
Angela Monteith

Contents

Sushi 寿司 6
- **Nigiri-zushi** 握り寿司 7
- **Maki-zushi** 巻き寿司 14
- **Other Sushi** その他の寿司 15

Noodles 麺類 16
- **Ramen** ラーメン 17
- **Udon, Soba** うどん、そば 19

Rice Dishes ご飯もの 22
- **Donburi** どんぶり 23
- **Other Rice Dishes** その他のご飯もの 25

Tabletop Grill/Hot Pot Cuisine
鉄板焼き／焼肉／鍋物 28
- **Teppan-yaki** 鉄板焼き 29
- **Yakiniku** 焼肉 30
- **Hot Pot Dishes** 鍋料理 31

Izakaya 居酒屋 33
- **Standard Dishes** 定番メニュー 34
- **Grilled Food** 焼き物 38

Boiled Food 煮物 41
Deep-fried Food 揚げ物 43
Japanese Pickles 漬物 46
Alcoholic Beverages 酒類 47
Non-alcoholic Beverages ソフトドリンク 49
Flour-based Dishes 粉物 50
Soup 汁物 51

Special Occasions イベント料理 52
Bento 弁当 55

Mochi/Sweets 餅／和菓子 56

Secret Ingredients かくし味 62
Soup stock 出汁 63
Flavorings 調味料 64
Condiments 薬味 65

Local Cuisine 都道府県別 郷土料理 67

Sushi

寿司

Sushi is one of Japan's most iconic culinary creations, offering a rich blend of tradition, flavor, and artistry. From high-end sushi bars to casual *kaitenzushi* (conveyor belt sushi), the dining experience varies greatly, catering to every budget and occasion. High-end sushi restaurants offer an intimate atmosphere, where chefs prepare each piece with precision, often using premium, seasonal ingredients. The dining experience focuses on quality, presentation, and interaction with the chef, making it ideal for special occasions. Sushi toppings, or "*neta*," include delicacies like tuna, salmon, squid, and sea urchin, each with unique flavors and textures that reflect the season and region. The proper way to enjoy sushi is to dip the fish side, rather than the rice, into the soy sauce.

While sushi is made with vinegared rice, *sashimi* is a simple dish of fresh fish or meat sliced thinly and served on its own, highlighting the natural flavors of the fish. At sushi restaurants, customers often start by ordering *sashimi* as an appetizer to enjoy with their drinks. After that, they move on to a selection of sushi.

Sushi

Nigiri-zushi 握り寿司

Tuna *Maguro* マグロ

Tuna, or *maguro*, is one of the most prized sushi toppings, known for its rich flavor and versatility. The meat is categorized into three main types based on fat content: *akami* (lean), *chutoro* (medium-fatty), and *otoro* (highly fatty). *Akami* offers a clean, meaty taste, while *chutoro* adds tenderness while chewing. *Otoro*, with its marbled texture and melt-in-your-mouth quality, is the most luxurious. Tuna is available year-round, but its peak season varies depending on the species and region. Often regarded as the "king of sushi," *maguro* is a must-try for both beginners and seasoned sushi enthusiasts alike.

Types of Tuna

Lean *Akami*

Highly fatty *Otoro*

Medium fatty *Chutoro*

Parts of Tuna

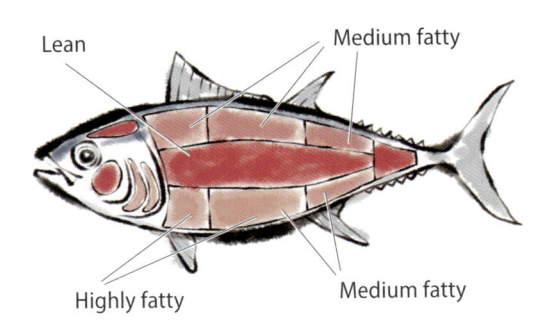

Lean

Medium fatty

Highly fatty

Medium fatty

Salmon *Sake* サーモン

Salmon is characterized by its rich, fatty flavor and smooth texture. Its vibrant orange color adds visual appeal. While not a traditional sushi ingredient in Japan, it is now widely appreciated around the world. Available in all seasons, it pairs perfectly with *wasabi*, soy sauce, or lemon.

Yellowtail *Hamachi* ハマチ

Hamachi, or young yellowtail, is a popular sushi topping with a rich, buttery flavor. It's best enjoyed in winter, at peak season, when the fish is fattier. It's a versatile fish, also delicious grilled or as *sashimi* (raw fish without rice).

Greater Amberjack *Kanpachi* カンパチ

Kanpachi is known for its moderate fat content and mild, refined flavor. The flesh has a translucent appearance and a firm, springy texture. Its peak season is summer, when the fish develops a perfect balance of fat and *umami*. It does not come across as overly fishy, making it an ideal choice for those new to sushi.

Horse Mackerel *Aji* アジ

Aji, or horse mackerel, is a popular sushi topping known for its mild yet savory flavor. Fresh *aji* offers a firm, springy texture with a perfect balance of meatiness and fat. It pairs well with ginger and green onions, which enhance its delicate taste and aroma.

Squid *Ika* イカ

Ika, or squid, is a classic sushi topping with a mild flavor and slightly chewy texture. Fresh *ika* has a subtle sweetness that is enhanced with a touch of soy sauce. Its simple yet elegant taste makes it a favorite among many sushi lovers.

Octopus *Tako* タコ

Made with a thin slice of poached octopus, *tako* sushi is somewhat chewy but tender. Its slightly sweet flavor pairs well with the seasoned rice underneath. Sometimes brushed with a soy sauce glaze, it offers visitors an authentic and delightful sushi experience.

Egg *Tamago* 玉子

Tamago nigiri, or egg sushi, is characterized by its sweet flavor and fluffy texture. Beaten eggs are seasoned with *dashi* and sugar, then rolled in layers in a special rectangular omelet pan. The delicate sweetness of *tamago nigiri* make it a popular choice for children or the end of a sushi meal.

Shrimp *Ebi* エビ

Ebi is prized for its sweet flavor and firm, bouncy texture. It's served either raw or cooked. Boiling enhances its vibrant red color, making it visually appealing. Larger shrimp, chilled to further enhance their sweetness, give a sumptuous experience. Its mild taste makes it a favorite across all audiences.

Scallop *Hotate* ホタテ

Hotate, or scallop, is known for its succulent sweetness and soft, silky texture. The scallop is butterflied to fit over the rice and sometimes topped with *yuzu kosho*, a spicy Japanese citrus paste. At its peak in winter, fresh *hotate* melts in your mouth, releasing layers of *umami* with every bite.

Sushi

Sea Bream *Tai* タイ

Tai, or sea bream, features a delicate flavor and a firm, refined texture. Fresh *tai* has a beautiful, translucent flesh that satisfies at every bite. Its peak season is spring, especially the prized "*sakuradai*," or (cherry) red sea bream. *Tai* is also served grilled or raw on special occasions.

Freshwater Eel *Unagi* ウナギ

Unagi, or freshwater eel, is known for its rich, buttery flavor and tender, fluffy texture. Grilled with a sweet-savory sauce, its smoky aroma is irresistible. Considered a summer delicacy, it's famously enjoyed on "*Doyo no Ushi no Hi*," the day of the ox in mid-summer.

Saltwater Eel *Anago* アナゴ

Anago, or saltwater eel, is less fatty than *unagi*, offering a mild, refined sweetness and a soft, delicate texture. Often grilled with a sweet-savory sauce or lightly salted, it gives out a pleasing aroma. Easy to digest, *anago* is a traditional topping in *Edo-mae*, or Tokyo-style sushi.

Flounder *Hirame* ヒラメ

Hirame, or flounder, is a premium whitefish with a delicate flavor and firm, smooth texture. Its peak season is winter, when the fish becomes richer and more flavorful. Often enhanced with methods like *kombu-jime* (kelp curing), *hirame* offers a refined and elegant taste, making it a standout choice for sushi.

Sea Urchin *Uni* ウニ

Uni, or sea urchin, is a premium sushi topping prized for its rich sweetness and creamy texture. Fresh *uni* offers a delicate ocean aroma and deep succulent flavor, especially at its peak in summer. To fully appreciate its refined taste, minimal soy sauce is recommended.

Fish Roe *Ikura* イクラ

Ikura, or salmon and trout roe, is recognized for its vibrant orange color and bursting, bubble-like texture. Seasoned with salt or soy sauce, it delivers a rich, savory flavor with a hint of sweetness. Roe is lushest in autumn, but the stunning color and unique texture of *ikura* sushi can be enjoyed year-round.

Kaitenzushi (Conveyor belt sushi)

Kaitenzushi

In contrast to the intimate atmosphere of an up-scale sushi bar, *kaitenzushi* (conveyor belt sushi) is a fun, affordable option where plates of sushi rotate on a conveyor belt. The belt often circles a middle island where the sushi is being prepared. *Kaitenzushi* restaurants are perfect for families, groups, or those looking for a quick, casual meal. While the quality may be simpler compared to high-end sushi places, the variety and convenience of *kaitenzushi* are appealing. In addition to raw fish sushi, these restaurants usually offer plates of cooked fish or meat. There is something for everyone at *kaitenzushi*.

Sushi is not just a meal but an experience that celebrates Japanese culture and the joy of sharing food. Don't miss out!

Up-scale sushi bar

Maki-zushi 巻き寿司

Certain types of sushi are deeply woven into Japanese culture, often enjoyed on specific holidays and celebrations. *Futo-maki* (thick rolled sushi) is associated with *Setsubun*, an early spring holiday, while *Chirashi-zushi* (layered sushi) is often served on *Hinamatsuri* (Doll's Festival), a holiday which celebrates the health and happiness of girls. Other rolled sushi, such as *temaki-zushi* (hand-rolled sushi), *hoso-maki* (thin rolled sushi), and *inari-zushi* (stuffed *tofu* pouch sushi) may be included in meals anytime, including picnics and lunchboxes.

Thick Rolled Sushi
Futo-maki 太巻き

Futo-maki is a thick sushi roll made by wrapping several ingredients with vinegared rice in *nori* (seaweed). Common fillings include *tamago* (Japanese omelet), cucumber, seasoned *shiitake* mushrooms, and sweet pink fish flakes, creating a visually appealing variety of colors.

Thin Rolled Sushi
Hoso-maki 細巻き

Hoso-maki is a thin sushi roll made with a single ingredient wrapped in vinegared rice and *nori* (seaweed). Common fillings include cucumber, *ume* (pickled plum), or *tekka* (tuna sashimi), offering simple and clean flavors. Its small, bite-sized pieces make it perfect for a light meal or as a palate cleanser.

Hand-rolled Sushi *Temaki-zushi* 手巻き寿司

Temaki-zushi (hand-rolled sushi) is a cone-shaped sushi roll made by wrapping vinegared rice and fillings in *nori* (seaweed). With ingredients like tuna, salmon, crab sticks, and vegetables, it's versatile and perfect for casual meals or home parties. While it is available in sushi restaurants, *temaki-zushi* is more commonly made and enjoyed at home with family or friends.

Other Sushi その他の寿司

Stuffed Tofu Pouch Sushi *Inari-zushi* いなり寿司

Inari-zushi is made by stuffing vinegared rice into sweet and savory fried *tofu* pouches. It has a unique sweetness and a soft, tender texture. While plain vinegared rice is standard, some variations include rice with sesame seeds or vegetables mixed in. Easy to make and portable, *inari-zushi* is a popular choice for lunchboxes and picnics.

Layered Sushi *Chirashi-zushi* ちらし寿司

Chirashi-zushi is a layered dish starting with vinegared rice on the bottom. Toppings such as seafood, egg strips, and vegetables are scattered across the rice to make a colorful presentation. The toppings range from lavish *sashimi* (raw fish) and *ikura* (fish roe) to simple homemade ingredients.

Noodles

麺類

Japanese noodle dishes, including *ramen*, *udon*, and *soba*, are staples of Japanese cuisine, each with its own unique flavor and cultural significance. *Ramen*, for example, offers diverse styles such as *shoyu* (soy sauce), *miso* (fermented soybean paste), *shio* (salt), and *tonkotsu* (pork bone) based broths. Each region boasts its own take on *ramen*, from the rich *miso ramen* of Sapporo to the creamy *tonkotsu ramen* of Kyushu. *Udon*, known for its thick, chewy texture, is featured in dishes like *kitsune udon*, topped with sweet fried *tofu*, and *tempura udon*, served with crispy *tempura*. *Soba*, made from buckwheat, is used in dishes like *mori soba*, served with dipping sauce, and *tempura soba*, which combines *soba*'s refreshing taste with the richness of *tempura*.

These noodle dishes are not just meals but cultural experiences, reflecting Japan's regional diversity, seasonality, and culinary artistry. For visitors, sampling these noodles is a delicious way to connect with Japanese traditions. Whether it's the bold flavors of *ramen* or the light elegance of *soba*, there's a noodle dish for everyone to enjoy.

Noodles

Ramen ラーメン

Soy Sauce Ramen *Shoyu Ramen* 醤油ラーメン

Shoyu (soy sauce) *ramen* is a classic *ramen* characterized by its salty dark brown broth. Common toppings include *chashu* (braised pork) and bamboo shoots. Regional variations offer unique flavors, showcasing Japan's delicate *umami*. It's a must-try dish for anyone visiting Japan.

Pork Bone Broth Ramen *Tonkotsu Ramen* とんこつラーメン

Tonkotsu ramen is known for its rich, creamy broth made by simmering pork bones for many hours. Originating in Kyushu, it pairs perfectly with thin noodles and is often topped with red pickled ginger and mustard greens. *Ramen* fans looking for bold, hearty flavors should not miss having a bowl of *tonkotsu ramen*.

Salt Broth Ramen *Shio Ramen* 塩ラーメン

Shio ramen features a clear, salt-based broth and is loved for its light, refreshing taste. Commonly made with chicken or seafood stock, it's topped with staples like green onions, bamboo shoots, and *chashu* (braised pork). Its simple, delicate flavors make it perfect for those seeking a lighter *ramen* option.

Miso Ramen *Miso Ramen* 味噌ラーメン

Miso ramen features a rich, flavorful broth made with fermented soybean paste. Originating in Sapporo, it's often topped with butter, corn, and stir-fried vegetables, making it a comforting choice during colder seasons. It's perfect for those who are hungering for a satisfying meal.

Dipping Noodles *Tsukemen* つけ麺

Tsukemen is a style of *ramen* where noodles and broth are served separately. The rich broth, often based on fish or pork, is paired with thick, chewy noodles. This dish combines warm soup with chilled noodles, offering a unique texture and flavor experience.

Cold Noodles *Hiyashi Chuka* 冷やし中華

Hiyashi Chuka is a chilled noodle dish popular in summer. Topped with colorful ingredients like cucumber, ham, egg, and tomato, it's served with a soy sauce or sesame-based dressing. Its refreshing flavor satisfies the palate in hot weather.

Noodles

Udon, Soba うどん、そば

Fried Tofu Udon *Kitsune Udon* きつねうどん

Kitsune Udon is a classic noodle dish featuring *udon* topped with sweet and savory simmered fried *tofu*. The warm *dashi* (broth) flavor pairs perfectly with the gentle sweetness of the *tofu*, creating a simple yet satisfying meal. This Kansai specialty gets it name from the color of the *tofu*—a light brown, like the fur of a *kitsune* (fox).

Raw Egg Udon *Tsukimi Udon* 月見うどん

Tsukimi Udon is a warm *udon* dish topped with a raw egg, named for its resemblance to the moon ("*tsukimi*" means moon-viewing). The egg blends with the broth, creating a rich and creamy flavor. Simple yet nutritious, it's a comforting and easy-to-enjoy meal.

Tempura Udon *Tempura Udon* 天ぷらうどん

Tempura Udon is a warm *udon* dish topped with crispy *tempura*, typically shrimp or vegetables. The combination of the savory *dashi* broth and the light crunch of *tempura* creates a perfect harmony. It's a satisfying and distinctly Japanese meal, offering a touch of indulgence.

Beef/Pork Udon *Niku Udon* 肉うどん

Niku Udon is a warm *udon* dish topped with sweet and savory simmered beef or pork. The meat's rich flavor infuses the broth, creating a hearty and flavorful dish. Filling and satisfying, it's especially popular during colder seasons.

Curry Udon *Curry Udon* カレーうどん

Curry Udon is a unique *udon* dish served in a savory, *dashi*-infused curry broth. It combines the spiciness of curry with the rich *umami* of Japanese flavors, creating a richly satisfying meal. It's a top choice for colder days or when you're craving a filling dish.

Hot Buckwheat Noodles *Kake Soba* かけそば

Kake soba is a simple and comforting Japanese noodle dish featuring buckwheat noodles in a light soy-based broth. Served hot, the clear *dashi* soup highlights the natural flavor of the *soba*. Often garnished with green onions, *kake soba* is a wholesome meal enjoyed year-round, but is traditionally served on New Year's Eve.

Cold Buckwheat Noodles *Mori Soba* もりそば

Mori Soba is a simple Japanese dish featuring chilled *soba* (buckwheat) noodles served on a bamboo tray, accompanied by a dipping sauce. The sauce, made from soy sauce and *dashi*, offers a rich and savory flavor. Light and refreshing, it's especially popular during hot weather.

Cold Noodles *Somen* そうめん

Somen is a traditional Japanese dish consisting of thin white wheat noodles served chilled with a *dashi* and soy dipping sauce. The dish is often garnished with green onions or ginger. Light and refreshing, *somen* is a perfect dish for hot summer days.

Pan-Fried Noodles *Yakisoba* 焼きそば

Yakisoba is a popular Japanese dish made with wheat-based noodles stir-fried with vegetables and meat, then flavored with a savory sauce. Common ingredients include cabbage and pork, often topped with pickled ginger and seaweed flakes. It's a favorite at festival stalls and a staple in home cooking.

Rice Dishes

ご飯もの

Japanese rice dishes offer a delicious variety that reflects the country's culinary diversity and cultural richness. From comforting *donburi* (rice bowls), like *tempura*-topped *tendon* or savory *gyudon*, to simple yet satisfying meals like *tamago kake gohan* (raw egg over rice), each dish showcases a unique way to enjoy rice as a staple food.

Rice bowls like *unadon*, with its grilled eel and sweet sauce, or *kaisendon*, featuring fresh *sashimi*, highlight Japan's premium ingredients, while casual dishes like *onigiri* and curry rice are perfect for a quick, filling meal. Even creative twists like *hayashi* rice (hashed beef over rice) and *omu* rice (rice-filled omelet) blend Japanese flavors with Western influences, illustrating the versatility of rice in Japanese cuisine.

These dishes are not only beloved in Japanese households but also highly recommended for visitors seeking to understand the role of rice in everyday life. Whether you're enjoying a hearty meal or a light snack, Japanese rice dishes offer a perfect balance of flavor, texture, and tradition, making them an integral part of the country's culinary identity.

Rice Dishes

Donburi　　　　　　　　　　　　どんぶり

Tempura Rice Bowl *Tendon* 天丼

Tendon is a traditional rice bowl topped with freshly fried *tempura* and drizzled with a sweet and savory sauce. Common *tempura* pieces include shrimp and seasonal vegetables, with the crispy batter perfectly complementing the flavorful sauce. It's a satisfying and convenient way to enjoy authentic Japanese flavors.

Pork Cutlet Rice Bowl *Katsudon* カツ丼

Katsudon is a popular rice bowl featuring a crisply fried pork cutlet simmered with eggs in a slightly sweetened *dashi* broth and served over rice. The broth enhances the flavors of the pork and eggs, creating a delicious combination. Filling and flavorful, it's a staple in Japanese home cooking and casual dining.

Chicken and Egg Rice Bowl *Oyakodon* 親子丼

Oyakodon is similar to *Katsudon* in that the ingredients are simmered with eggs in a sweet and savory *dashi* broth and served over rice. However, small chunks of chicken are used instead of a pork cutlet, which creates a delightful play on words since *"oyako"* means parent and child. With its tender eggs and flavorful broth, it's a oft-requested meal in Japanese homes.

Beef Rice Bowl
Gyudon 牛丼

Gyudon is a simple and popular rice bowl dish featuring thinly sliced beef and onions simmered in a sweet and savory sauce, served over rice. Loved for its convenience, it's a staple in homes and can also be found at chain restaurants. Pickled ginger is usually piled on top of the meat, enhancing the flavor of this filling dish even further.

Eel Rice Bowl
Unadon 鰻丼

Unadon is a luxurious rice bowl featuring grilled eel glazed with a sweet and savory sauce. It's especially popular in summer as a stamina-boosting meal. The rich flavor of the sauce perfectly complements the tender texture of the eel.

Seafood Rice Bowl *Kaisendon* 海鮮丼

Kaisendon is an elegant rice bowl topped with fresh *sashimi*, such as tuna, salmon, and salmon roe. Often seasoned with *wasabi* and soy sauce, it offers a delightful way to enjoy the bounty of the sea and is very popular with tourists.

Rice Dishes

Other Rice Dishes　　その他のご飯もの

Japanese Mixed Rice　*Takikomi Gohan*　炊き込みご飯

Takikomi Gohan is a traditional Japanese dish in which the rice is cooked together with ingredients like mushrooms, chicken, and carrots. A *dashi* broth infuses the rice with a rich aroma and flavor. Often featuring seasonal ingredients, it's a simple yet flavorful comfort food in Japanese cuisine.

Tea over Rice　*Ochazuke*　お茶漬け

Ochazuke is a traditional dish in which tea or *dashi* broth is poured over rice and topped with ingredients like seaweed, pickles, or salmon. Easy to prepare and gentle on the stomach, it's commonly enjoyed as a light meal or a late-night snack. Its simplicity offers a uniquely satisfying flavor.

Egg over Rice　*Tamagokake Gohan*　卵かけご飯

Tamagokake Gohan is a simple yet popular dish made by cracking a raw egg over freshly cooked rice and mixing it with soy sauce. Despite its simplicity, it offers a rich, creamy flavor and is cherished as a quick and nutritious meal in busy Japanese households.

Rice Soup *Zosui* 雑炊

Zosui is a warm dish made by simmering rice in *dashi* or other broth along with ingredients like eggs, vegetables, and chicken. Often enjoyed as a finishing dish after hot pot meals, it's flavorful and easy to digest. Its comforting taste is the perfect end to a satisfying meal.

Red Bean Rice *Sekihan* 赤飯

Sekihan, or red bean rice, is a traditional Japanese dish made by steaming sticky rice with *azuki* beans, which give the rice its reddish color. It's often served on celebratory occasions like birthdays or weddings, symbolizing good fortune. Typically topped with black sesame seeds and salt, it offers a subtly sweet flavor.

Rice Ball *Onigiri* おにぎり

Onigiri, or rice balls, are a classic Japanese food made by shaping a lump of salted rice by hand and wrapping it in seaweed. Fillings like pickled plum, salmon, or tuna salad are popular, offering a variety of flavors. Convenient and portable, *onigiri* is a favorite for lunches and quick snacks.

Curry over Rice *Curry Rice* カレーライス

Curry rice is a beloved dish based on the "meat and potatoes" version of Indian curry developed by the British. Common ingredients such as beef, pork, or chicken, are boiled along with potatoes, carrots, and onions. Curry roux is added to make a thick, mildly spiced gravy. Known for its rich and slightly sweet flavor, it's a staple in homes and even school lunches across Japan.

Hashed Beef over Rice *Hayashi Rice* ハヤシライス

Hayashi rice is a Japanese-style Western dish made with thinly sliced beef and onions simmered in a rich tomato-based sauce. Its hearty and flavorful taste makes it as popular as its sister dish, curry rice, enjoyed by both children and adults in homes across Japan.

Rice-filled Omelet *Omu Rice* オムライス

Omu rice is a Japanese-style Western dish consisting of ketchup-seasoned chicken rice wrapped in a fluffy omelet. It's often decorated with designs or messages made with ketchup. Some restaurants serve versions with different sauces. When cooked at home, children love the original ketchup-topped version.

Tabletop Grill/ Hot Pot Cuisine

鉄板焼き／焼肉／鍋物

Japanese cuisine offers an incredible range of dining experiences, and among the most engaging are *teppan-yaki*, *yakiniku*, and hot pot dishes. These styles of cooking not only highlight the diverse flavors of Japan but also bring people together around a shared table, creating moments of connection and enjoyment.

Teppan-yaki, often prepared on an iron griddle right before your eyes, combines the thrill of live cooking with the sumptuousness of perfectly grilled meats, seafood, and vegetables. *Yakiniku*, Japan's take on Korean barbecue, lets diners grill bite-sized portions of marinated meat at their table, savoring each piece fresh off the grill. Hot pot dishes, on the other hand, center around simmering pots of broth, where diners cook fresh ingredients like vegetables, *tofu*, and thinly sliced meat, each bite steeped in rich, comforting flavors.

Whether it's the theatrical flair of *teppan-yaki*, the hands-on fun of *yakiniku*, or the warming camaraderie of a hot pot meal, these dishes showcase the heartwarming and interactive spirit of Japanese cuisine.

Tabletop Grill/Hot Pot Cuisine

Teppan-yaki 鉄板焼き

Teppan-yaki is renowned for its use of high-quality, luxurious ingredients, with beef, abalone, and spiny lobster taking center stage. Juicy, marbled Japanese beef, often from famous *wagyu* breeds, is expertly grilled to bring out its rich, savory flavor and melt-in-your-mouth texture. Abalone, prized for its firm bite and delicate sweetness, is seared to perfection, enhancing its natural marine taste. Spiny lobster, with its vibrant color and tender, sweet meat, adds an elegant touch to the meal.

These ingredients are not only delicious but also embody the essence of Japanese cuisine: a deep respect for natural flavors and a meticulous approach to preparation. *Teppan-yaki* combines these premium foods with the excitement of live cooking, creating a memorable dining experience that delights all the senses.

Spiny lobster

Abalone

Beef

Yakiniku 焼肉

Japanese *yakiniku* is a unique way to enjoy beef, with each cut offering distinct flavors and textures. Tender and marbled sirloin melts in your mouth, delivering a rich, savory taste, while *kalbi* (short ribs) are prized for their juicy, flavorful fat and smoky aroma. For a leaner option, *rosu* (loin) provides a light yet satisfying taste, highlighting the natural flavor of the meat. *Gyutan* (beef tongue) offers a slightly chewy texture and a refreshing, mild flavor. Paired with a variety of sauces and cooked to perfection, *yakiniku* showcases the diversity and depth of Japanese culinary artistry.

Premium Loin
Gokujo Rosu

Chuck Tender
Togarashi

Tri-tip Cut
Tomosankaku/Mikazuki

Sirloin
Saroin

Top Blade
Misuji

Parts of Beef

Hot Pot Dishes 鍋料理

Meat and Vegetable Hot Pot *Sukiyaki* すき焼き

Sukiyaki is a traditional hot pot dish featuring thinly sliced beef and vegetables simmered in a sweet and savory soy-based sauce. Common ingredients include Chinese cabbage, leeks, *tofu*, and *shirataki* (konjac) noodles. The rich flavors are enhanced by dipping each bite into raw egg, making it a popular choice for warm, communal meals with family and friends.

Shabu-shabu *Shabu-shabu* しゃぶしゃぶ

Shabu-shabu is an enjoyable hot pot dish where thin slices of beef or pork are briefly swished in hot *kombu* broth before eating. It's enjoyed with dipping sauces like *ponzu* (Japanese citrus sauce) or sesame sauce, along with vegetables and *tofu*. Known for its light texture and healthy appeal, it's served at special s*habu-shabu* restaurants or easily made at home.

Chicken Vegetable Hot Pot *Mizutaki* 水炊き

Mizutaki is a hot pot dish with chicken and vegetables simmered in water to bring out the natural flavors of the ingredients. The broth is flavorful yet light, and ingredients are often dipped into *ponzu* (Japanese citrus sauce) or sesame sauce. It's a comforting dish, especially popular during the cold months when families gather around the table eating communally from a *nabe* (ceramic pot.)

Offal Hot Pot *Motsunabe* もつ鍋

Motsunabe is a hot pot dish made with beef or pork offal, simmered with vegetables in a rich, delicious broth. The dish is typically seasoned with garlic and chili peppers, creating a hearty and spicy taste. A filling and warming meal, *motsunabe* is especially popular in winter.

Mixed Meat and Seafood Hot Pot *Yosenabe* 寄せ鍋

Yosenabe is a hot pot dish that combines a variety of seafood, meat, and vegetables. The broth infuses the flavors of all the ingredients, making each bite rich and satisfying. A popular choice for both family and group meals, *yosenabe* offers the flexibility to choose a wide range of ingredients, making it pleasing to everyone.

Tofu Hot Pot *Yudofu* 湯豆腐

Yudofu is a traditional Japanese hot pot dish where *tofu* is gently simmered in *kombu* (dried kelp) broth and enjoyed with *ponzu* (Japanese citrus sauce), as well as other condiments. It's a simple yet healthy dish, easy to digest, and especially popular during winter. The cooking method highlights the natural flavors, allowing you to savor the *tofu*'s smooth texture and delicate taste.

Izakaya

居酒屋

An *izakaya* is a traditional Japanese pub where people gather to enjoy food and drinks in a casual and lively atmosphere. *Izakayas* serve a wide variety of dishes, such as *sashimi*, *yakitori*, *tempura*, and *edamame*, and drinks like beer, *sake*, or *shochu*. Unlike Western-style pubs, *izakayas* emphasize shared dining, with small plates designed for sharing among friends or colleagues.

The experience typically begins with an *otoshi*, a small appetizer that is served automatically alongside the first drink. This is the equivalent of a seating charge, and is generally not optional. Ordering is flexible, and customers can enjoy a relaxed pace, ordering as they go. *Izakayas* are popular for after-work gatherings, known as *nomikai*, where coworkers bond over drinks and conversation.

Seating varies from bar counters to *tatami* rooms, creating a warm and inviting atmosphere. Whether you're looking for a quick drink or a leisurely meal with friends, *izakayas* offer a unique insight into Japanese culture and hospitality, making them a must-visit for anyone exploring Japan.

Standard Dishes

定番メニュー

Edamame *Edamame* 枝豆

Edamame are young soybeans boiled or steamed in their pods and are a common Japanese snack. They can be easily eaten by hand and are especially popular as a companion to beer. Rich in nutrients, *edamame* are packed with protein and dietary fiber, making them a healthy and well-loved appetizer.

Sashimi *Sashimi* 刺身

Sashimi is a traditional Japanese dish made with thinly sliced raw fish or shellfish. It is not only enjoyed in sushi restaurants but can often be found on *izakaya* menus. There, *sashimi* is often served as a standalone dish, but sushi is typically not offered. In smaller *izakayas*, the fish will change daily and can be found on the specials board, so ask the server what is available that day.

Japanese-style Omelet *Dashimaki Tamago* だし巻き玉子

Dashimaki tamago is a Japanese omelet made by rolling layers of eggs mixed with *dashi* (broth) into a fluffy, tender texture. The balance of sweetness and saltiness creates a delicate flavor, and it's often served in *izakayas* or restaurants as a dish to accompany drinks.

Lightly-seared Bonito
Katsuo no Tataki カツオのタタキ

Katsuo no tataki is made by thinly slicing lightly-seared bonito fillets. The outer surface is charred while the inside remains raw. It's often served with *ponzu* (Japanese citrus sauce) and garnished with scallions, garlic, or ginger. This dish offers a delightful balance of *umami* and smokiness and is especially popular in the summer.

Sliced Cucumber with Miso *Morokyu* もろきゅう

Morokyu is a simple and refreshing snack made by mixing sliced cucumber with salt and *miso*. The rich flavor of *miso* complements the crisp texture of the cucumber, creating a perfect balance. It's a popular appetizer in *izakayas* and pairs well with beer or *sake*.

Potato Salad *Potato Sarada* ポテトサラダ

Japanese-style potato salad is a staple both in home cooking and on *izakaya* menus. The boiled potatoes are partially mashed and combined with a creamy mayonnaise dressing. Raw vegetables such as cucumbers and carrots are added for their crunch and flavor, and pre-made versions often contain ham.

Savory Egg Custard *Chawan-mushi* 茶碗蒸し

Chawan-mushi is a savory egg custard, known for its smooth texture. Infused with a delicate *dashi* broth, it typically contains ingredients such as chicken, shrimp, and mushrooms, and has a subtle sweetness and *umami*. It's an essential dish in traditional Japanese meals, such as set meals and *kaiseki* cuisine.

Chilled Silken Tofu *Hiyayakko* 冷奴

Hiyayakko is a simple dish made with chilled silken *tofu* topped with green onions, ginger, and bonito flakes, and seasoned with soy sauce. It has a refreshing taste, making it a perfect appetizer or light snack during hot weather.

Deep-fried Tofu *Agedashi Tofu* 揚げ出し豆腐

Agedashi tofu is made by dusting cubes of *tofu* with potato starch, then deep-frying until crispy on the outside and soft on the inside. It's served in a warm *dashi*-based broth and topped with grated *daikon*, green onions, and bonito flakes. It's warming with a refreshing taste, and is popular year-round.

Raw Octopus Marinated in Wasabi *Takowasa* たこわさ

Takowasa is a simple and spicy snack, made by mixing octopus *sashimi* with *wasabi* and soy sauce. The texture of the octopus and the sharpness of the *wasabi* create a perfect balance, making it an excellent pairing with beer or *sake*.

Vinegared Mozuku Seaweed *Mozuku-su* もずく酢

Mozuku-su is a refreshing dish made by mixing *mozuku* seaweed with vinegar. The acidity of the vinegar complements the unique texture of the *mozuku*, offering a light and clean taste. Known for its health benefits, it's especially during popular the summer and is said to stimulate the appetite.

Japanese Cucumber Salad
Kyuri no Sunomono きゅうりの酢の物

Kyuri no sunomono is made by mixing thinly sliced cucumbers with vinegar, sugar, and salt. The crunchy texture of the cucumber balanced with the tang of the vinegar makes it a great appetizer or side dish to enhance any Japanese meal.

Grilled Food 焼き物

Grilled Chicken Skewers
Yakitori 焼き鳥

Yakitori is a classic Japanese dish made by skewering and grilling chicken. It's typically seasoned with either salt or a sweet soy-based sauce, and different parts of the chicken offer various textures and flavors. Common types include thigh meat, *negima* (chicken with leek), and *tsukune* (chicken meatballs). Often found in *izakayas* and at street stalls, it is a popular, easy-to-eat food that is often enjoyed with beer.

Teriyaki *Teriyaki* 照り焼き

Teriyaki is made by grilling chicken or fish and glazing it with a sweet and salty sauce. The sauce, made from soy sauce, *mirin*, and sugar, is reduced to a shiny glaze that coats the meat or fish. It has a rich, flavorful taste and is commonly eaten with white rice.

Grilled whole Squid *Ika no Sugatayaki* イカの姿焼き

Grilled whole squid, or *ika no sugatayaki*, is a simple dish where the whole squid is grilled, offering a crispy exterior and tender, juicy interior. It's often served with salt or lemon, allowing the natural *umami* of the squid to shine through. Popular in *izakayas* and seaside eateries, it's a favorite for seafood lovers.

Grilled Pacific Saury
Sanma no Shioyaki サンマの塩焼き

Grilled Pacific saury, or *sanma no shioyaki*, is made by lightly salting the whole fish and grilling it. The skin becomes crispy and fragrant while the flesh stays tender and juicy, allowing you to enjoy its rich *umami*. It's a quintessential dish that represents the flavors of autumn in Japan.

Grilled Mackerel *Saba no Shioyaki* サバの塩焼き

Grilled mackerel, or *saba no shioyaki*, is a flavorful dish where the fillets of mackerel are salted and grilled. The outer skin becomes crispy, while the inside remains moist and tender, highlighting the rich taste of the fish. It pairs perfectly with rice and is a common dish in Japanese home cooking and set meals.

Grilled Salmon *Sake no Shioyaki* サケの塩焼き

Grilled salmon, or *sake no shioyaki* consists of lightly salted grilled salmon fillets. Using only salt, the *umami* of the fatty salmon is enhanced and can be enjoyed without complicated seasonings. A fixture in Japanese cooking, it's often eaten with rice and *miso* soup.

Grilled Atka Mackerel *Yaki Hokke* 焼きほっけ

Grilled *hokke*, or *yaki hokke*, is a staple fish dish in Japan. The fish is cut open and grilled, and generally only seasoned with salt to highlight the natural taste. The flesh is tender and flaky, with a rich, fatty flavor.

Grilled Black Cod in Miso
Gindara no Saikyoyaki 銀鱈の西京焼き

Grilled black cod with *saikyo miso* is a dish where black cod is marinated in sweet *saikyo miso* and then grilled. The rich sweetness and flavor of the *miso* infuse the fish, complementing the tender, flaky texture of the cod. The grilling enhances the aroma, making it a perfect dish to enjoy with rice.

Gyoza *Gyoza* 餃子

Gyoza are dumplings filled with pork and vegetables and are typically pan-fried or steamed. The crispy skin and juicy filling are the key features, with garlic and ginger enhancing the flavor. In Japan, *gyoza* are often enjoyed as an appetizer with beer or served alongside rice.

Izakaya

Boiled Food   煮物

Japanese Hot Pot *Oden* おでん

Oden is a traditional Japanese dish that is usually eaten in winter. It's made by simmering various ingredients, such as *daikon* radish, eggs, konjac, and fish cakes in a flavorful broth. The rich, warm broth soaks into the ingredients, creating a simple yet deeply satisfying flavor. It's the perfect dish for cold weather and can be found in many *izakayas* and convenience stores

Simmered Yellowtail and Daikon Radish
Buri Daikon ブリ大根

Buri daikon is made by simmering yellowtail fish and *daikon* radish in a sweet and savory broth. The rich fat of the fish and the tender texture of the *daikon* create a perfectly balanced flavor. This dish is especially popular in the winter and is typically eaten with rice.

Meat and Potato Stew *Nikujaga* 肉じゃが

Nikujaga is a comforting home-cooked dish made by simmering beef or pork with potatoes and onions in a sweet and savory broth. The ingredients absorb the rich flavors of the broth, creating a hearty and flavorful meal. Both warming and filling, it's popular in Japanese home cooking.

Miso-simmered Mackerel *Saba no Misoni* サバの味噌煮

Miso-simmered mackerel, or *saba no misoni*, is a traditional Japanese dish where mackerel is simmered in a *miso*-based sauce. The rich *umami* of the *miso* blends perfectly with the fatty mackerel, creating a deeply flavorful dish. It's usually enjoyed with rice and is a beloved comfort food in Japanese households.

Simmered Flounder *Karei no Nitsuke* カレイの煮付け

Simmered flounder, or *karei no nitsuke*, is a a classic dish where flounder is cooked in a sweet and savory sauce made with soy sauce, *mirin*, and sugar. The tasty broth seeps into the delicate fish, enhancing its mild taste.

Braised Pork Belly *Buta no Kakuni* 豚の角煮

Braised pork belly, or *buta no kakuni*, is a dish where pork belly is slow-cooked in a sweet and savory sauce, making the meat tender and rich in flavor. The fat melts into the sauce, creating a deep *umami* taste. It's a hearty and satisfying dish that is often eaten with rice.

Izakaya

Deep-fried Food 揚げ物

Tempura *Tempura* 天ぷら

Tempura is a popular Japanese dish where seafood and vegetables are coated in batter and deep-fried. The crispy texture of the light batter highlights the natural flavors of the ingredients. Typically served with dipping sauce or salt, *tempura* is usually enjoyed alongside rice, *soba* or *udon*.

Japanese-style Fried Chicken *Tori no Karaage* 鳥の唐揚げ

Karaage is a popular Japanese dish where chicken is coated in batter and deep-fried until crispy on the outside and juicy on the inside. It's seasoned with garlic and ginger for extra flavor. Often served as an appetizer with beer or as a side with rice, *karaage* is loved in both *izakayas* and homes.

Deep-fried Chicken Cartilage
Nankotsu no Karaage ナンコツの唐揚げ

Nankotsu no karaage, or deep-fried chicken cartilage, has a crispy exterior and a unique, crunchy texture inside. Typically seasoned with salt or lemon, it pairs wonderfully with beer or *sake* and is a staple of *izakaya* menus.

Deep-fried Skewers *Kushikatsu* 串カツ

Kushikatsu is a dish where meat and vegetables are skewered, coated in breadcrumbs, and deep-fried. Usually served with a variety of dipping sauces, the contrast between the crispy exterior and juicy interior is particularly enjoyable. Famous in Osaka, it's commonly enjoyed in *izakayas* and at street stalls.

Pork Cutlet *Tonkatsu* トンカツ

Tonkatsu, or deep-fried breaded pork cutlet, is popular throughout Japan. The outside is crispy, while the inside remains tender. It's typically enjoyed with a special sauce and shredded cabbage, and is often served as a topping for curry or as part of a set meal.

Croquette *Korokke* コロッケ

Korokke is a staple Japanese dish made by coating mashed potatoes or ground meat in breadcrumbs and deep-frying until crispy on the outside and fluffy on the inside. It's typically served with sauce and is often enjoyed at home and in bento boxes.

Izakaya

Deep-fried Horse Mackerel *Aji Furai* アジフライ

Aji fry is a dish where horse mackerel is coated in breadcrumbs and deep-fried. The natural flavor of the fish shines through, and it's often served with tartar sauce or lemon. It's a popular dish enjoyed with rice or beer.

Deep-fried Shrimp *Ebi Furai* エビフライ

Ebi fry is a classic Japanese dish where shrimp is coated in breadcrumbs and deep-fried. The plump juiciness of the shrimp contrasts wonderfully with the crispy exterior. It's usually served with tartar sauce and is often found in Japanese set meals and bento boxes.

Japanese Pickles　　　　　　　　　漬物

Pickled Daikon Radish
Takuan たくあん

Takuan is a pickle made by fermenting salted *daikon* radish. It has a unique blend of sweetness and tartness, and is often enjoyed as a side dish. *Takuan* is a staple in Japanese home cooking and set meals.

Traditional Japanese pickles *Nukazuke* ぬか漬け

Nukazuke is a traditional style of pickling, where vegetables are fermented in rice bran. Common ingredients include cucumbers, eggplants, and *daikon* radish, which develop a unique flavor during the fermentation process.

Pickled Japanese Shallot
Rakkyo らっきょう

Rakkyo is a type of small onion pickled in sweet vinegar. It has a crunchy texture and a sweet-and-sour flavor, and is often served with curry or as an accompaniment to drinks.

Pickled Plum　*Umeboshi* 梅干し

Umeboshi are traditional Japanese pickled plums made by salting and drying *ume* fruit under the sun. Known for their sour and salty taste, they are often enjoyed with rice. *Umeboshi* are also considered healthy and hold an essential place in Japanese food culture.

Alcoholic Beverages 酒類

Sake *Nihonshu* 日本酒

Sake is a traditional Japanese alcoholic beverage made from rice. It's brewed by fermenting rice with yeast, creating a wide range of flavors from sweet to dry. There are various types of *sake*, and it can be enjoyed either chilled or heated, depending on personal preference. *Sake* pairs exceptionally well with Japanese cuisine, enhancing the flavors of the meal.

Beer *Biiru* ビール

Japanese beer is light and easy to drink, with lager being the most common type. It has a crisp taste and is usually poured with a large head of foam.

Distilled Japanese Spirit *Shochu* 焼酎

Shochu is a distilled spirit made from rice, barley, or sweet potatoes, with a high alcohol content. It's enjoyed neat, on the rocks, or with water, and is particularly popular in Kyushu.

Sour, Chuhai
Sawa, Chuhai サワー、酎ハイ

Sours and *chuhai* are popular Japanese drinks made with *shochu* as the base. They are typically mixed with fruit juices like lemon, lime, or grapefruit, offering a refreshing taste. Easy to drink, they are a staple of *izakaya* menus.

Highball *Highball* ハイボール

Highballs in Japan are typically made from whisky and soda water. The refreshing taste can be enjoyed on its own or with food.

Distilled Okinawan spirit
Awamori 泡盛

Awamori is a distilled spirit from Okinawa, made primarily from rice. It has a high alcohol content and a distinct flavor. Typically enjoyed neat, on the rocks, or with water, it pairs well with Okinawan cuisine.

Plum liquor *Umeshu* 梅酒

Umeshu is a Japanese fruit liquor made by steeping *ume* plums in alcohol and adding sugar. It has a sweet and sour flavor, typically enjoyed on the rocks or mixed with soda. It's often served as a dessert drink at the end of a meal.

Non-alcoholic Beverages ソフトドリンク

Oolong tea *Uron Cha* 烏龍茶

Oolong tea is a Chinese tea made from partially fermented leaves, offering a refreshing flavor with a hint of sweetness. It's commonly consumed during meals in Japan, and can be enjoyed both hot and cold.

Calpis® *Karupisu* カルピス

The origin of Calpis goes back more than 100 years when company founder Kaiun Mishima traveled to Mongolia and was served a fermented horse milk drink. He was impressed with its tangy flavor and health-giving properties. Today, Calpis is made using fermented milk (cow's not horse's!) and is slightly sweetened for a refreshing taste.

Tea *Ocha* お茶

Tea is a popular drink in Japan, with varieties like green tea, *hojicha* (roasted green tea), and *genmaicha* (brown rice green tea). It has a refreshing taste and is commonly consumed with meals. Tea is also perfect for relaxing, making it an essential part of Japanese culture.

Flour-based Dishes 粉物

Japanese Savory Pancake *Okonomiyaki* お好み焼き

Okonomiyaki is made by mixing cabbage, pork, and seafood with batter, then cooking it on a hot plate. Topped with sauce and mayonnaise, the ingredients and toppings can be endlessly customized. Osaka and Hiroshima are well known for it, and many specialty restaurants can be found in both cities.

Hiroshima-style Okonomiyaki *Hiroshimayaki* 広島焼き

Hiroshima-style *okonomiyaki* is a variation where the ingredients are layered rather than mixed. It includes cabbage, pork, bean sprouts, and noodles, all topped with a special sauce. This unique cooking style results in a hearty, filling dish.

Takoyaki *Takoyaki* たこ焼き

Takoyaki originates from Osaka and is made by cooking batter with octopus and green onions in round molds. The resulting balls have a crispy exterior and soft interior, and are typically topped with sauce, mayonnaise and seaweed flakes.

Monjayaki *Monjayaki* もんじゃ焼き

Monjayaki is a Tokyo specialty made by mixing chopped ingredients with a thin batter and cooking it on a hot plate. It has a crispy exterior and soft, gooey interior and is often topped with sauce. It's perfect for sharing with friends or family.

Soup 汁物

Miso Soup *Miso Shiru* 味噌汁

Miso shiru is a traditional Japanese soup made by dissolving *miso* in *dashi* broth and adding ingredients like *tofu*, seaweed, and green onions. It's a staple in daily meals, enjoyed for its warmth and health benefits.

Pork and Vegetable Miso Soup *Ton Jiru* 豚汁

Ton jiru is a home-cooked soup made by simmering pork and vegetables in a *miso*-based soup. Common ingredients include *daikon*, carrots, and potatoes which offer a rich and warming flavor. It's a perfect dish for the colder seasons.

Clear Soup *Osuimono* お吸い物

Osuimono is another traditional Japanese soup, made with a delicate, clear *dashi* broth and simple ingredients like seaweed, *tofu*, and *shiitake* mushrooms. Known for its subtle flavor, it's an essential dish in Japanese course meals.

Vegetable Soup *Kenchin Jiru* けんちん汁

Kenchin jiru is a hearty vegetable soup made with *tofu*, *daikon*, carrots, and burdock root in a soy sauce-based broth. Originating from Zen temples, it's a healthy, meat-free dish perfect for warming up in cold weather.

Special Occasions

イベント料理

In Japanese culture, food plays a significant role in special events and celebrations. These dishes are often imbued with meanings of good luck, prosperity, and health. For example, *osechi ryori*, enjoyed on New Year's Day, features a variety of dishes symbolizing wishes for a fortunate year ahead. *Kaiseki* and *shojin* cuisine are often served at formal gatherings, reflecting a deep appreciation for seasonal ingredients and cultural traditions. Moreover, dishes like *toshikoshi soba*, *oden*, *makunouchi bento*, and *ekiben* carry special meanings and are enjoyed during festive occasions. Food served on special occasions not only offer rich flavors but also reflect traditional culture and history, turning shared meals into moments of significance with loved ones.

Special Occasions

Celebratory Meal *Kaiseki Ryori* 会席料理

Kaiseki is a multi-course meal featuring seasonal ingredients, often enjoyed during special occasions and celebrations, such as weddings, birthdays, New Year's, and tea ceremonies. The beautifully presented dishes are meant to be savored slowly, allowing diners to appreciate both the flavors and the seasonal elements. *Kaiseki* is also served at high-end restaurants and *ryotei* (traditional Japanese inns) and is perfect for welcoming important guests.

Vegetarian Meal *Shojin Ryori* 精進料理

Shojin cuisine is based on Buddhist principles, focusing on plant-based ingredients like vegetables, *tofu*, and seaweed, without the use of animal products. It emphasizes purity of mind and body, with careful attention to the choice of ingredients and cooking methods. Typically served in temples or during tea ceremonies, it's enjoyed during spiritual practices or quiet moments. *Shojin* cuisine remains popular today for its healthy and balanced approach to eating.

New Year's Meal *Osechi Ryori* おせち料理

Osechi ryori is a traditional Japanese meal served on New Year's Day, with each dish symbolizing wishes for longevity, prosperity, and health. The meal typically includes black beans, red and white *kamaboko* (fish cakes), *datemaki* (sweet rolled omelet), and simmered dishes, all arranged in a layered box. It is enjoyed with family and friends to celebrate the new year. *Osechi* is an integral part of Japanese culture and New Year's traditions.

Mochi Soup *Zoni* 雑煮

Zoni is a warm soup with rice cakes, and its ingredients and seasoning vary by region and family. Common ingredients include chicken, radish, and carrots, simmered in a flavorful broth. It's a traditional dish especially enjoyed during the New Year's celebration.

New Year's Noodle Soup *Toshikoshi Soba* 年越しそば

Toshikoshi soba is a traditional Japanese dish eaten on New Year's Eve, symbolizing longevity and the removal of bad luck. It typically consists of long noodles, which represent long life, served in a warm broth with toppings like green onions and *tempura* crumbs. It's a simple yet meaningful dish enjoyed with family and friends to mark the end of the year.

Special Occasions

Bento 弁当

Traditional Lunchbox
Makunouchi Bento 幕の内弁当

Makunouchi bento is a traditional Japanese lunchbox filled with grilled fish, simmered vegetables, *tamagoyaki* (Japanese omelet), and pickles. Originally made for theater-goers and eaten during *makunouchi* (intermission), the rice and other ingredients are bite-sized for efficient eating. Today, it's enjoyed by people of all ages in various settings, such as offices, picnics, and schools.

Train Station Lunchbox *Ekiben* 駅弁

Ekiben are lunchboxes sold at train stations, designed for easy eating while traveling. They often feature local specialties and regional dishes, allowing travelers to experience the local food culture. *Ekiben* is a beloved part of the travel experience in Japan.

Homemade Lunchbox *Tezukuri Bento* 手作り弁当

Homemade *bento* is a lunchbox filled with dishes prepared at home. It typically includes rice, meat or vegetable side dishes, and *tamagoyaki* (Japanese omelet), arranged attractively in a small box. Often taken to school or work, it's a comforting reminder of love from home.

Mochi/Sweets

餅／和菓子

Mochi and *wagashi* (traditional Japanese sweets) are deeply tied to Japan's seasons and cultural celebrations. *Mochi*, made from glutinous rice, has a chewy texture and is enjoyed in various forms, such as grilled or boiled, during New Year's events or festivals. *Wagashi* are made from ingredients like red bean paste, rice flour, and agar, with an emphasis on visual appeal and seasonal themes. *Sakura mochi*, *ohagi*, and *yokan* evoke the essence of Japanese culture and the changing seasons. *Wagashi* are often enjoyed with tea, and is also popular as gifts or souvenirs. Both *mochi* and *wagashi* are a part of everyday life but also add a special touch to important moments, making them a cherished part of Japanese culinary traditions.

Mochi/Sweets

Grilled Mochi *Yaki Mochi* 焼き餅

Grilled *mochi* is made by toasting rice cakes until crispy on the outside and chewy inside. It's often enjoyed with soy sauce and is a seasonal treat, especially during the New Year's holiday.

Seaweed Mochi *Isobe Mochi* 磯部餅

Isobe mochi is a simple Japanese snack made by wrapping grilled *mochi* in *nori* (seaweed) and drizzling it with soy sauce. The savory seaweed and soy sauce complement the sweetness of the *mochi*. It's commonly enjoyed during the New Year holiday or as a light snack.

Roasted soybean flour Mochi *Kinako Mochi* きな粉餅

Kinako mochi is made by coating *mochi* with *kinako* (roasted soybean flour). The nutty flavor of *kinako* complements the chewy texture of the *mochi*. Often sweetened with sugar, it's commonly enjoyed with tea.

Oak Leaf Wrapped Mochi *Kashiwa Mochi* 柏餅

Made by wrapping *mochi* in oak leaves spread with red bean paste, *Kashiwa mochi* is traditionally eaten on Children's Day in May. While the leaves are not eaten, their aroma complements the chewy texture of the *mochi*.

Cherry Leaf Wrapped Mochi *Sakura Mochi* 桜餅

Sakura mochi is made by wrapping *mochi* in a completely edible pickled cherry blossom leaf. It has the fragrant aroma and slight saltiness of the leaf, spread with sweet red bean paste. It's commonly enjoyed in spring when the *sakura* come to full bloom.

Mugwort Mochi *Kusa Mochi* 草餅

Kusa mochi is a type of *mochi* made with *yomogi* (mugwort), giving it a fragrant aroma and mild bitterness. It's filled with sweet red bean paste and is commonly enjoyed in spring.

Kudzu Jelly Mochi *Kuzu Mochi* くず餅

Kuzu mochi is a chewy sweet made from kudzu starch, known for its translucent, jelly-like texture. It's typically served with black syrup and *kinako* (roasted soybean flour) and is especially refreshing during the summer.

Mochi/Sweets

Rice Dumpling Sticks
Mitarashi Dango みたらし団子

Mitarashi dango is made by coating skewered rice dumplings with a soy sauce and sugar sauce. The sweet and savory flavor of the sauce offers a perfect balance of sweetness and *umami*.

Strawberry Mochi *Ichigo Daifuku* いちご大福

Ichigo daifuku is made by wrapping fresh strawberries and red bean paste in soft *mochi*. The chewy *mochi*, combined with the tart, juicy strawberry and lightly sweet bean paste create a perfect balance, making it a popular treat in the spring.

Fruit Mochi *Furutsu Daifuku* フルーツ大福

Fruit *daifuku* is an offshoot of *ichigo daifuku*, with various kinds of sweet fruit wrapped in red bean paste and soft *mochi*. After *ichigo daifuku* became popular in the 1980s, other fruit was substituted, so now there is a different type of *daifuku* for every season. Try kiwi *daifuku* in the summer, grape *daifuku* in the fall and mandarin orange *daifuku* in the winter.

Red Bean Paste Rice Balls *Ohagi* おはぎ

Ohagi is made with sticky rice, usually coated with red bean paste or rolled in powdered soybeans. The rice inside symbolizes hope for a bountiful harvest, while the red bean paste is said to ward off evil. It's commonly eaten during the autumn equinox and is known for its chewy texture and sweetness.

Red Bean Paste Jelly with Fruit *Anmitsu* あんみつ

Anmitsu is a dessert made with agar jelly, fruit, and red bean paste, often served with black syrup. The chewy texture of the jelly and sweetness make it a popular summer treat.

Bean Paste Bun *Manju* まんじゅう

Manju is a sweet made by wrapping red bean paste in dough. The soft dough and sweet filling create a balanced flavor, making it a popular tea snack or souvenir.

Bean Paste Cake *Dorayaki* どら焼き

Dorayaki is a Japanese sweet made with soft sponge cakes filled with red bean paste. The combination of sweet filling and soft cake makes it a popular and convenient snack.

Stuffed Waffle *Taiyaki* たい焼き

Taiyaki is a fish-shaped pastry, traditionally filled with red bean paste, though modern versions include *matcha*, custard, and chocolate. It has a crispy exterior and a soft, chewy interior. Made on a special cast iron mold, similar to a waffle iron, it's a popular and convenient snack often sold at street stalls.

Mochi/Sweets

Stuffed Wafers *Monaka* もなか

Monaka is a Japanese sweet made by sandwiching red bean paste between thin wafers. The wafers are crunchy, while the filling is mildly sweet, offering a simple yet flavorful snack.

Gelled Sweet Bean Paste *Yokan* 羊羹

Yokan is a traditional Japanese sweet made primarily from red bean paste, with agar added to give it a firm texture. Its rich sweetness and long shelf life make it a popular choice for gifts or as a tea accompaniment.

Rice Crackers *Senbei* せんべい

Senbei is a traditional Japanese snack made from rice, typically seasoned with salt or soy sauce and baked into a crisp texture. It comes in a variety of flavors, from sweet to savory, and is popular as a tea snack or souvenir.

Rice Cracker Snack Mix *Kaki no Tane* 柿の種

Kaki no tane is a spicy rice snack, often sold in bags mixed with peanuts. It has a light, crunchy texture and a savory flavor, making it a popular snack or beer accompaniment.

Secret Ingredients

かくし味

In Japanese cuisine, there are many "hidden flavors" that add depth and complexity to dishes. These secret ingredients not only enhance the flavor, but also bring out the natural taste of any food they are added to.

For example, *dashi*, made from *kombu* and bonito flakes, creates the base *umami* that gives stews and soups, and *miso* soup such a rich depth. Flavorings like soy sauce, *miso*, and vinegar add necessary saltiness and acidity, balancing the meal. These background ingredients elevate even the simplest dishes, conveying a sense of seasonality and regionality. Understanding these hidden flavors is essential to appreciating the essence of Japanese cuisine.

Secret Ingredients

Soup stock 出汁

Dried Kelp *Kombu* 昆布

Kombu is a seaweed rich in glutamic acid, essential for making *dashi* in Japanese cuisine. *Kombu dashi* is used in soups and stews, and *miso* soup, adding depth and richness. Dried *kombu* is commonly used not only for *dashi* but also as a base for simmered and clear soups.

Bonito Flakes *Katsuobushi* カツオぶし

Katsuobushi is dried, smoked bonito, a traditional ingredient. It has a rich *umami* flavor and aroma, commonly used for making *dashi* or as a topping on dishes like *okonomiyaki*. It is similar to *kombu* in that it creates a unique base for *dashi*, giving a taste of the sea to dishes, without being overly fishy.

Tiny Dried Fish *Niboshi* 煮干し

Niboshi are small, dried fish, typically sardines, used primarily to make *dashi*. They have a strong *umami* flavor and fishy aroma, adding depth to soups and stews, and *miso* soup. *Niboshi* provides a simple yet robust flavor profile to dishes.

Flavorings 調味料

Soy Sauce *Shoyu* しょうゆ

Soy sauce is a Japanese seasoning made from fermented soybeans and wheat, known worldwide for its salty *umami* taste. It enhances the flavor of various dishes and comes in many varieties, such as low sodium.

Japanese Vinegar *Osu* お酢

Japanese vinegar is a liquid made from fermented rice or wheat, with acetic acid as its main component. It has a tangy flavor and enhances plainer dishes. It's often used in sushi, pickles, and as a preservative.

Sweet rice Wine *Mirin* みりん

Mirin is a sweet seasoning that is becoming more common even outside of Japan. Made from rice, rice malt, and alcohol, it adds a unique sweetness and a glossy finish to dishes, playing an essential role in enhancing the flavor of simmered foods and sauces.

Cooking Sake *Ryori-shu* 料理酒

Cooking *sake* is a type of alcohol used to add depth and *umami* to dishes. It's commonly used in stews, stir-fries, and fish dishes, enhancing the overall flavor of the food.

Soybean Paste *Miso* みそ

Miso is a fermented paste made from soybeans, known for its rich *umami* and salty taste. It's used in *miso* soup, stews, and sauces, with varieties like red and white *miso*.

Secret Ingredients

Condiments 薬味

Green Onions *Negi* ねぎ

Negi (green onions) is a garnish used in Japanese cuisine, known for its aroma and texture. It enhances dishes like *miso* soup, *udon*, and grilled fish, and is said to stimulate the appetite.

Japanese Perilla Leaf *Shiso* しそ

Shiso is a fragrant herb with a refreshing flavor, commonly used as a garnish for *sashimi*, *tempura*, and sushi. Its lovely shape and color add a touch of beauty to any food presentation.

Japanese Horseradish
Wasabi わさび

Wasabi is a spicy condiment commonly served with *sashimi* and sushi. Its sharp, pungent kick is an essential part of enjoying raw fish dishes.

Japanese Ginger *Myoga* ミョウガ

Myoga is a leafy herb bud with uniquely colored layers. It is often used as a garnish for cold dishes or vinegared foods. It's milder than regular ginger, but has a peppery bite.

Grated Japanese Radish
Daikon Oroshi 大根おろし

Grated *daikon* is a condiment known for its light, tangy flavor. It's commonly served with grilled fish, *tempura*, and *udon*, and is also known to aid digestion.

The Correct Way to Hold Chopsticks

Japanese food is most often eaten with chopsticks. In ancient times chopsticks resembled tweezers, being made from a split strip of bamboo. Today's practice of using two separate sticks apparently dates to the Nara period (710–794), while *waribashi* (disposable chopsticks) were introduced during the Edo period (1603–1868). Traditionally, eating was intimately linked with religious ritual so there were various rules governing table manners. These included how to hold chopsticks, and even now many families are vigilant about teaching this to children.

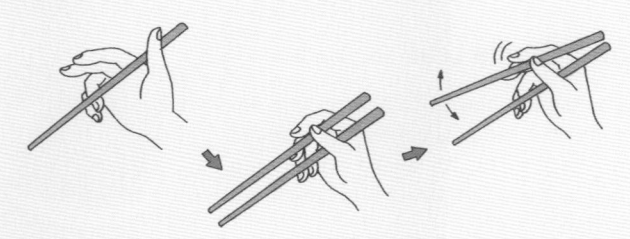

① One chopstick is secured between the ball of the thumb and the tip of the ring finger.

② The other is held between the tip of the thumb and tip of the middle finger, and steadied by the index finger above.

③ Move the middle and index fingers up and down to pick up food.

Basic Japanese Phrases

Before you pick up your chopsticks, here are some useful food-related phrases. Unlike English, Japanese is a phonetic language, so you say exactly what you see without stress on any syllable. (*kore=koh-reh, arigatou=ah-ree-gah-toh*) But don't worry too much about pronunciation. Most Japanese are just happy to hear their language, no matter how it sounds.

What do you recommend?	*O-susume wa nan desu ka?*	おすすめは何ですか？
(Grace before eating)	*Ita-daki masu.*	いただきます。
(Appreciation after eating)	*Gochi-so sama deshita.*	ごちそうさまでした。
What is this?	*Kore wa nan desu ka?*	これは何ですか？
It's delicious.	*Oishii desu!*	おいしいです！
Excuse me.	*Sumi-masen.*	すみません。
Thank you.	*Arigatou gozai masu.*	ありがとうございます。
I'm allergic to …	*… no arerugii ga arimasu.*	…のアレルギーがあります。

Local Cuisine

都道府県別 郷土料理

[Hokkaido]
Grilled Mutton *Jingisukan* ジンギスカン

A grilled dish featuring mutton or lamb marinated in a special sauce and cooked on a convex cast iron pan. *Jingisukan* was named after the famed Mongolian emperor, Genghis Khan. The meat is cooked on the raised center of the hat-shaped pan, while vegetables, such as sliced green peppers and cabbage, are placed in the 'brim' of the hat to catch the juices from the meat as they cook. Hokkaido, the large northern island of Japan, is home to many cattle and sheep farms.

[Aomori]
Rice Cracker Soup *Senbei Jiru* せんべい汁

A dish where *Nanbu senbei*, crackers made from wheat flour and salt, are broken into a flavorful soup filled with meat, fish, mushrooms, and vegetables. The crackers stay firm and add an extra heartiness to the soup, perfect on a cold day in Aomori, northern Honshu.

[Iwate]
Dumpling Stew *Mamebu Jiru* まめぶ汁

A soy sauce-based stew flavored with dried sardines and *kombu* broth, containing local vegetables, grilled *tofu*, and "*mamebu*" —small dumplings stuffed with sugar-coated walnuts. Young people who have moved away come back to Iwate yearning for *Mamebu jiru*, it is said.

[Miyagi]
Edamame Paste Mochi *Zunda-mochi* ずんだ餅

A simple yet refined paste made by boiling freshly harvested *edamame*, carefully peeling the thin skins, and mashing them before adding a touch of sugar and salt. The paste is perched atop a freshly made *mochi* for a unique Japanese treat. *Zunda* paste is said to have originated when *samurai* used the hilt of their swords to grind *edamame*. They then ate the paste as-is for a quick burst of energy before battle.

Local Cuisine

[Akita]
Roasted Rice Hot Pot *Kiritanponabe* きりたんぽ鍋

A hot pot soup in which roasted mashed rice is simmered with local chicken, burdock root, mushrooms, leeks, and other ingredients in a chicken-based broth. *Kiritanpo* is said to have originated in a time when locals went on long hunting trips. They used leftover rice by mashing it onto cedar sticks and roasting the sticks by the fire. Since Akita Prefecture, located along the Sea of Japan coast, is famous for its delicious rice, this dish is often served after a new crop has been harvested.

[Yamagata]
Taro Soup *Imoni* いも煮

A hot pot dish featuring ingredients like *taro*, konjac, leeks, beef, and burdock root, simmered in a broth seasoned with sugar, *sake*, and soy sauce. This soup is so popular in Yamagata that one city has a whole festival centered around it. The main event is cooking a huge amount of *Imoni* in a 6-meter wide cauldron. Construction cranes are used to mix the ingredients and it is served to as many as 30,000 attendees!

[Fukushima]
Squid and Carrot Marinade *Ika Ninjin* いかにんじん

A side dish made by finely slicing dried squid and carrots, then marinating them in a sweet and savory sauce made with soy sauce and coarse sugar or *mirin*. Historically made in winter as the marinating process preserved the ingredients for a long time, it is now served year-round in a meal with rice or as a snack with *sake*.

[Ibaraki]
Monkfish Hot Pot *Ankonabe* あんこう鍋

A hot pot dish that uses the entire monkfish, a fish known for its "no-waste" nature. The dish is simmered with monkfish liver, *miso*, and vegetables for a rich and flavorful experience. During the Edo period (1603–1868), fishermen would make *ankonabe* on the boat for themselves in order to save the more pricey fish for customers.

[Tochigi]

Utsunomiya Gyoza *Utsunomiya Gyoza* 宇都宮餃子

These fried dumpings are packed with vegetables like green onions, garlic chives, and cabbage, with a mild amount of garlic for a light and approachable flavor. Utsunomiya is the capital of Tochigi Prefecture and also known as the '*Gyoza* Capital of Japan.'

[Gunma]

Himokawa Noodle *Himokawa Udon* ひもかわうどん

As Gunma Prefecture has always been a large wheat producing part of Japan, it's no wonder that noodles are a traditional part of the region's cuisine. *Himokawa* noodles are unique in that they are very thin and very wide—up to 10 cm! Simmered in savory broth with seasonal vegetables, this *udon* dish is hearty and delicious.

[Saitama]

Pork Cutlet Rice Bowl
Warajikatsudon わらじカツ丼

Saitama Prefecture, northwest of Tokyo, boasts its own version of *katsudon* (pork cutlet rice bowl) featuring an impressively large cutlet. It's so big, one might mistake it for a straw sandal, the precise translation of *waraji*. The pork 'sandal' is dipped in a generous amount of a secret sauce for an unforgettable flavor.

[Chiba]

Chopped Mackerel
Namero なめろう

A fisherman's dish made by finely chopping fresh *aji* (horse mackerel) and mixing it with *miso*, minced green onions, and ginger, then pounding the mixture until it becomes sticky. The name comes from '*nameru*' in Japanese, meaning 'to lick.' It is said the more you lick the plate of *namero*, the better it tastes.

Local Cuisine

[Tokyo]
Clam Mixed Rice *Fukagawameshi* 深川めし

A dish of *miso* or soy sauce-simmered clams, green onions, *tofu*, and other ingredients served over rice for a comforting meal. During the Edo Period (1603–1868), large mud flats appeared at low tide in what is now Tokyo Bay. Clams were abundant and this simple dish was prepared and sold at food stalls to busy fishermen and workers in the area.

[Kanagawa]
Whitebait Rice Bowl *Nama Shirasudon* 生しらす丼

A dish featuring translucent *nama shirasu* (raw whitebait), topped with condiments such as seaweed, green onions, and *shiso* leaves, and enjoyed with soy sauce over rice. *Shirasu* is plentiful off the coast of the Shonan Peninsula south of Yokohama. Fishermen there catch *shirasu* and sell them quickly to ensure freshness.

[Yamanashi]
Dumpling Miso Soup *Hoto* ほうとう

Yamanashi Prefecture, upon which part of Mount Fuji lies, has never been a rice-growing region. This may be why noodles are more popular there than rice. *Hoto* noodles are said to be more like dumplings than *udon*. Simmered in a *miso*-based broth with seasonal vegetables such as pumpkin, cabbage and mushroom, this dish is warm and filling on a cold winter's day.

[Nagano]
Carp Miso Soup *Koikoku* 鯉こく

A traditional *koi* (carp) dish featuring large slices of carp simmered in *miso* soup. Carp in Saku City, Nagano are raised in freshwater streams and are therefore light and fluffy compared to carp from rice paddies. This classic *miso*-based stew has been enjoyed on New Year's day in Saku City for generations.

[Niigata]
Bamboo Leaf Dumpling *Sasa Dango* 笹団子

One in the unique lineup of *wagashi* (Japanese sweets), *sasa dango* is a dumpling filled with plenty of mugwort and wrapped in *sasa* (broad bamboo leaves), which are said to have natural antibacterial properties. While in modern days it has become a type of dessert, it was a staple food during the Sengoku period (1477–1573).

[Toyama]
Firefly Squid with Vinegared Miso *Hotaruika no Sumisoae*
ほたるいかの酢味噌和え

Firefly squid, usually a deep-ocean breed, come to the shallows of Toyama Bay in the spring. There the squid starts glowing blue and white, giving them the name "the mystery of Toyama Bay." The squid are caught and boiled fresh, then dressed in a tangy *miso* vinegar sauce.

[Ishikawa]
Duck and Cracker Soup *Jibuni* じぶ煮

Various theories have emerged on the origin of *Jibuni*, but all agree that it was a dish consumed by *samurai* in the Edo period (1603–1868). Made with chicken or duck, seasonal vegetables, and wheat gluten crackers, it is characterized by its thick, velvety texture.

[Fukui]
Fermented Mackerel *Heshiko* へしこ

A fermented fish dish made by salting fish such as *saba* (mackerel) or sardines, then marinating them in rice bran and seasonings, allowing them to mature for a length of time. It was an important source of protein during the harsh winters of Fukui Prefecture in the mid-Edo period (18th century).

Local Cuisine

[Shizuoka]
Shizuoka Skewered Oden *Shizuoka Oden* 静岡おでん

Oden (Japanese hot pot) heralds the beginning of winter as it includes hearty ingredients in a warm, satisfying broth. Shizuoka natives skewer beef *tendon*, black *hanpen* (fish cakes), *daikon* radish, eggs, and other ingredients and simmer them in a dark broth. Once the skewers are removed from the broth, *aonori* (seaweed flakes) and *dashi* powder are sprinkled on top.

[Gifu]
Mochi Skewers with Miso *Gohei Mochi* 五平餅

A snack made by wrapping mashed rice around a skewer, coating it with a *miso* or soy sauce-based glaze, and grilling it to perfection. *Gohei mochi* originated long ago when lumberjacks and hunters worked long days in the mountains. People ate them as they prayed for safety away from home.

[Aichi]
Miso Noodle Soup *Misonikomi Udon* 味噌煮込みうどん

A hearty dish made by simmering firm *udon* noodles in a rich broth seasoned with nationally famous *Hatcho miso*. It includes chicken, fried *tofu*, egg, and green onions, offering excellent nutritional balance. The laborious process of making *Hatcho miso* has continued for over 350 years in the city of Okazaki, Aichi Prefecture.

[Mie]
Marinated Fish Sushi *Tekone-zushi* てこね寿司

A type of sushi made by marinating red fish *sashimi*, such as bonito or tuna, in a soy sauce-based marinade and serving it over vinegared rice. The popular dish originated along the Mie coastline where busy fishermen would cut *sashimi* out of freshly caught fish, marinate it for a few minutes, then place it on rice.

[Shiga]
Fermented Carp with Rice *Funa-zushi* ふなずし

One of the traditional forms of sushi, made by fermenting salted fish with rice. This method was originally developed to preserve fish for long periods without spoilage. It has long been used in Shiga Prefecture to cure stomachaches, due to the lactic acid produce during fermentation.

[Kyoto]
Herring Noodles *Nishin Soba* ニシンそば

A unique Kyoto *soba* dish featuring "*migaki nishin*" (dried herring) simmered in a light soy sauce and *kombu* (kelp) broth, served atop flavorful *dashi*-based hot *soba* noodles. Hokkaido has its own version of *Nishin Soba* which features a strongly flavored broth.

[Osaka]
Japanese Savory Pancake *Okonomiyaki* お好み焼き

A dish made by mixing finely chopped cabbage, meat, and seafood into a wheat flour batter, then grilling it on both sides on a hot plate like a pancake. It is served with toppings like sweet and savory sauce, mayonnaise, as well as *aonori* (seaweed flakes) and bonito flakes. While it is a popular home-cooked dish, *okonomiyaki* restaurants invite customers to make their own on the large grill in the middle of the table.

[Hyogo]
Akashi Grilled Egg Balls *Akashiyaki* 明石焼き

A snack made by mixing wheat flour, eggs, and *dashi* into a batter, adding pieces of octopus, and grilling it in a special pan. The resulting balls are then dipped into a bowl of *dashi*. Also known as *tamagoyaki* (grilled egg balls), it's a street food enjoyed by young and old alike.

Local Cuisine

[Nara]
Persimmon Leaf Sushi *Kakinoha-zushi* 柿の葉寿司

Pressed sushi made by wrapping salted mackerel or salmon with vinegared rice in *kakinoha* (persimmon leaves). After resting overnight, the aroma of the persimmon leaves and the *umami* of the fish infuse the rice, creating a unique and delicious flavor. It is thought *Kakinoha-zushi* was created as a moneymaker for Wakayama fishermen when they were required to pay a high annual tribute to their lords. They sold the sushi to nearby villages after the summer mackerel catch.

[Wakayama]
Mustard Green Riceball *Mehari-zushi* めはりずし

A large rice ball wrapped in salted *takana* (mustard greens), this regional sushi is popular as a souvenir and *ekiben* (train station *bento*). The name is especially quirky, having a meaning close to "eye-opening" sushi. It is said that *Mehari-zushi* looks so delicious, it makes your mouth, and therefore your eyes, open wide.

[Tottori]
Mixed Rice *Daisen Okowa* 大山おこわ

A colorful and healthy dish, *Daisen Okowa* is made by cooking rice with ingredients like *shiitake* mushrooms, burdock root, chestnuts, konjac, and fried *tofu*, seasoned with *dashi*, soy sauce, and sugar. It was served in the Meiji Period (1868–1912) at festivals and fairs near Daisen-ji, a Buddhist temple in Tottori Prefecture.

[Shimane]
Clam Soup *Shijimi Jiru* しじみ汁

A soup made with *shijimi* clams from Lake Shinji, seasoned with soy sauce or *miso*. The clams impart a rich, aromatic broth full of flavor. *Shijimi* clams were once so plentiful near Lake Shinji, elderly women would pull carts around the village selling them.

[Okayama]
Octopus Mixed Rice *Takomeshi* たこめし

A flavorful mixed rice dish made with *umami*-rich octopus from the Seto Inland Sea, whose calm waters and scenic islands prompts comparison to the Mediterranean. The octopus is roughly chopped with carrots and other ingredients, then cooked together with a soy sauce-based *dashi*, capturing the rich aroma of the sea.

[Hiroshima]
Hiroshima-style Okonomiyaki *Hiroshimayaki* 広島焼き

A dish made by cooking a thin, crepe-like batter, then layering it with cabbage, bean sprouts, pork belly, *yakisoba* noodles, and egg. Unlike Kansai-style *okonomiyaki*, the ingredients are assembled in layers rather than mixed together, making it a difficult 'pancake' to flip (and best left to professionals).

[Yamaguchi]
Pufferfish Sashimi
Fugusashi ふぐ刺し

A dish featuring thinly sliced *fugu* (pufferfish) *sashimi*. The firm texture gives it a pleasant chewiness, and the slices are cut so thin that the plate's design is visible, enhancing both the presentation and the flavor experience. The pufferfish's potential deadliness is taken very seriously in Japan and only certified chefs are allowed to cut and sell it.

[Tokushima]
Buckwheat Porridge
Sobagome Zosui そば米雑炊

A porridge made by simmering "*sobagome*" (buckwheat grains that have been boiled and dried) with vegetables and meat in a flavorful *dashi* broth. Because Tokushima is a mountainous region, rice does not grow well there and buckwheat became the staple crop. Usually ground to make flour, *Sobagome Zosui* features twice-boiled buckwheat seeds, yielding a high-protein, high-fiber meal.

Local Cuisine

[Kagawa]
Sanuki Noodles *Sanuki Udon* 讃岐うどん

Using high-quality wheat which traditionally was grown in Kagawa Prefecture (formerly known as Sanuki Prefecture), *Sanuki Udon* can be served cold with dipping sauce, or hot with various toppings. Of the top three types of *udon* in Japan, *Sanuki* is said to be the most popular, possibly due to its unique chewy texture.

[Ehime]
Sea Bream Mixed Rice *Tai-meshi* 鯛めし

A local specialty of Ehime Prefecture, *Tai-meshi* (sea bream rice) comes in two varieties: one in which a whole sea bream is cooked with rice, and another in which *sashimi* of sea bream is marinated in a special sauce, mixed with condiments, and served over rice. *Tai* has been part of Japanese history for centuries, being served as part of celebratory meals.

[Kochi]
Seared Bonito *Katsuo no Tataki* カツオのたたき

Kochi Prefecture boasts the highest bonito consumption in all of Japan. The fish are caught with poles and lines, rather than with nets, to prevent damage. Large fillets of bonito are set on a pitchfork-type grill and placed directly inside a flaming straw fire. The outside of the fillet is seared, absorbing the smoky aroma of the straw. *Ponzu* (Japanese citrus sauce) and a dash of salt draw out the unique flavor of the bonito.

[Fukuoka]
Chicken Hot Pot *Tori no Mizutaki* 鳥の水炊き

A hot pot dish featuring *tori* (chicken) simmered with its bones to create a rich, white broth, combined with seasonal vegetables and enjoyed with *ponzu* (Japanese citrus sauce). "*Mizutaki*" literally means 'cooked in water,' and this simple dish is one of the classic hot pots in Japan, rich in collagen and low in fat.

[Saga]
Thick Winter Stew *Noppei Jiru* のっぺい汁

A soup packed with ingredients like *taro*, burdock root, and konjac, characterized by its thickened broth, achieved by adding potato starch. It's a versatile dish, served at celebratory meals with chicken or strictly vegetarian at Buddhist ceremonies.

[Nagasaki]
Egg Noodle Soup with Vegetables *Chanpon* ちゃんぽん

While a bowl of *Chanpon* may look like *ramen*, it's actually composed of egg noodles and a variety of stir-fried vegetables and seafood. It's said to have originated in the early 20th century when a Chinese chef at a Nagasaki restaurant wanted to make a cheap yet delicious meal for some Chinese students there.

[Kumamoto]
Deep-Fried Lotus Root *Karashi Renkon* からし蓮根

A dish where lotus root holes are filled with a *miso* paste mixed with mustard, coated in a basic flour and egg yolk batter, and deep-fried to perfection. It is said to have originated in the early 17th century when a Hosokawa clan lord became very ill. A local monk discovered that lotus root could help, but the lord refused to eat it. So the monk made it irresistible with the *miso*-mustard mixture.

[Oita]
Dumpling Soup *Dango Jiru* だんご汁

Oita Prefecture on the island of Kyushu is a region of Japan where rice doesn't grown well, so wheat is more common. This *shiru* (soup) uses long, flat dumplings, made by kneading wheat flour into thin strips, in a *miso*-based broth cooked with seasonal vegetables. Barley *miso* is a popular choice in Kyushu.

Local Cuisine

[Miyazaki]
Fried Chicken with Tartar Sauce *Chikin Nanban* チキン南蛮

A nationally famous dish originating in the southern island of Kyushu, it features fried chicken tossed in a sweet and sour sauce. It's served with a generous topping of tartar sauce and a side of rice. Miyazaki natives consider this a 'soul food' of their region.

[Kagoshima]
Fish Paste Patties *Tsukeage* つけあげ

A dish made by mixing fish paste with *tofu* and Kagoshima *sake*, then deep-frying it. *Tsukeage* come in many shapes such as disks, balls, and fish. Burdock, boiled eggs, and other ingredients can be added for variety. Known as *satsuma-age* in other prefectures, It's widely enjoyed across Japan.

[Okinawa]
Pork Belly Noodle Soup *Soki Soba* ソーキそば

While most *soba* is made with buckwheat flour, this unique dish of the islands is made with wheat flour, producing off-white colored noodles. Served in a rich and flavorful broth made from pork bones and bonito flakes, it is typically topped with *soki* (simmered pork belly), stick-shaped fish cakes, and other classic garnishes.

WASHOKU
A Handbook of Japanese Food

2025年2月2日　第1刷発行

編　者	IBCパブリッシング
発行者	賀川洋
発行所	IBCパブリッシング株式会社 〒162-0804 東京都新宿区中里町29番3号 菱秀神楽坂ビル TEL 03-3513-4511 FAX 03-3513-4512 www.ibcpub.co.jp
印刷所	株式会社シナノパブリッシングプレス

©IBC Publishing, Inc. 2025

落丁本・乱丁本は小社宛にお送りください。
送料小社負担にてお取り替えいたします。
本書の無断複写（コピー）は
著作権法上での例外を除き禁じられています。

ISBN 978-4-7946-0859-8

Printed in Japan

English text by Raina Ruth Nakamura and Angela Monteith

Photographs:
PIXTA, Adobe Stock, photolibrary, photo AC